words of
hope
for
Women

Carolyn Larsen

Revell
a division of Baker Publishing Group
Grand Rapids, Michigan

© 2019 by Carolyn Larsen

Published by Revell
a division of Baker Publishing Group
PO Box 6287, Grand Rapids, MI 49516-6287
www.revellbooks.com

Printed in the United States of America

Library of Congress Cataloging-in-Publication Data
Names: Larsen, Carolyn, 1950– author.
Title: Words of hope for women / Carolyn Larsen.
Description: Grand Rapids : Revell, a division of Baker Publishing Group, 2019.
Identifiers: LCCN 2018055472 | ISBN 9780800736422 (pbk.)
Subjects: LCSH: Christian women—Religious life. | Bible—Meditations.
Classification: LCC BV4844 .L37 2019 | DDC 242/.643—dc23
LC record available at https://lccn.loc.gov/2018055472

19   20   21   22   23   24   25   7   6   5   4   3   2   1

1

Hope of Heaven

Praise be to the God and Father of our Lord Jesus Christ! In his great mercy he has given us new birth into a living hope through the resurrection of Jesus Christ from the dead, and into an inheritance that can never perish, spoil or fade. This inheritance is kept in heaven for you, who through faith are shielded by God's power until the coming of the salvation that is ready to be revealed in the last time.

1 PETER 1:3–5

How amazing is it that you have the hope of eternal life in heaven with Jesus? That hope for heaven doesn't mean it might or might not happen. Forever in heaven is a certainty if you have accepted Jesus as your Savior, because God raised Jesus from the dead. You're part of their family now. The promise of eternity is true, and it will never change. Heaven will be wonderful—forever! To be in God's presence in the beautiful glory of heaven, reunited with loved ones— what a glorious hope!

Another part of God's promise of hope is that he is keeping watch over you until you are promoted to the glory of heaven. Once you've been adopted into his family by your acceptance of Jesus, God promises you a place in his heaven forever. But you're not free-floating between now and then. God's power and love are watching over you. You don't ever have to be afraid of what life brings. You can call out to him for help whenever you need it. He's ready to fight for you!

2

Hope Comes from Trust

God remembered Noah and all the wild animals and the live-stock that were with him in the ark, and he sent a wind over the earth, and the waters receded.

GENESIS 8:1

od saved Noah from the flood that wiped out civilization as it was. He put Noah and his family on the ark where they rode out the storm. It must have been frightening. Did they hear the cries of those who died? Were the animals skittish with fear as the ark bounced around in the storm? Did it feel like they were on the ark forever? It had been 150 days. Did Noah have any communication from God in that time? Did he wonder if God remembered them? Noah had hope for the "what's next" in his life because God had assured him he would save him from the flood. He had hope because he trusted God.

How's your hope level these days? Do you trust God to remember what you're going through? Do you trust that his plan to rescue you or help you will actually come to fruition? Without trust there is no hope. Without relationship there is no trust. God did rescue Noah in his time and with his preordained plan. He will also rescue you in his time and with his plan. Keep your hope level high as you trust the One who promises to help you.

True Joy

May the God of hope fill you with all joy and peace as you trust in him, so that you may overflow with hope by the power of the Holy Spirit.

ROMANS 15:13

How do you define joy? What does it look like in your life? Joy is different from happiness, which is a fleeting emotion. Happiness is great, but it comes from experiences you have or interactions with people you enjoy. It comes and goes.

Joy comes from deep within your heart. It is not dependent on external circumstances. In fact, you can have joy even when your circumstances are unpleasant. That's because true joy comes from trusting God and knowing his love and care in your life. Your relationship with him is the source of joy because you have the power of his Holy Spirit available to give you strength to fight off temptations that compromise your decision to live for him. When you trust that the situations in your life are God's will for you, you know that the unpleasantness or unhappiness is only for the moment. Joy comes from your hope in God's good plan for you.

Hope in Fighting Temptation

No temptation has overtaken you except what is common to mankind. And God is faithful; he will not let you be tempted beyond what you can bear. But when you are tempted, he will also provide a way out so that you can endure it.

1 Corinthians 10:13

Temptation is hard to resist. It's . . . tempting. Whether you're fighting the temptation to eat one more chocolate chip cookie or to sleep in instead of getting up to exercise, it's hard. Some temptation goes deeper, like cheating on your taxes, cheating on your spouse, joining in a judgmental, critical assessment of another person . . . anything that takes you away from showing God's love to others by your obedience to him.

Satan throws temptation at you many times every day. Sometimes it's subtle, sometimes more obvious, but he is persistent because he knows constant temptation wears you down until you give in. His goal is to pull you away from God and make you believe you have failed him.

But even if you sometimes give in to temptation, it doesn't mean you've failed God! He loves you and will forgive you. You have the hope of victory because you have God! Cry out to him. Scream if you need to. Ask for his strength and power to help you withstand the temptation. God may not take the temptation away, but his strength will help you resist it and stay true to your faith in him.

5

Hope in God's Comfort

*He heals the brokenhearted
and binds up their wounds.*
PSALM 147:3

*P*erhaps you know someone who has suffered a broken heart. Heartbreak can be debilitating. A person who is grieving may be so lost in her grief that she withdraws from life. Staying home, not engaging with others, not eating . . . or eating too much. Maybe she can see no way out of the grief and no life beyond it. Getting through grief seems pretty hopeless for her. Maybe that someone is you . . . or has been at some point in your life.

You can find hope for restoration in trusting that God will help you pick up the pieces of your broken heart and make sense of life again. He will heal your wounds and help you through the pain of grief. God loves you, and while loss of relationships and physical death are a part of life, he will give you the strength to get through the pain. His comfort will give you a new lease on life. It may take time, but eventually you will begin to notice the sunshine again. You will join back into life with your family and friends.

Keep hoping in God's comfort and love. You won't be disappointed.

6

Ask and You Shall Receive

Ask and it will be given to you; seek and you will find; knock and the door will be opened to you. For everyone who asks receives; the one who seeks finds; and to the one who knocks, the door will be opened.

MATTHEW 7:7–8

If you're a control freak, these might be your dream verses. They sort of make it sound like you can ask God for anything you want and—*boom*—it's yours. Wouldn't that be quite a deal? Maybe, but it isn't what these verses promise. They actually promise something better. They offer the opportunity for you to let go. Stop trying to control your life; let go and let God control it.

These verses are promised to those who are walking closely with Christ. People who spend time each day reading and absorbing God's Word. People who are so submitted to God that his desires become their desires for their lives. Now these verses make sense. You can ask anything of God because your heart and mind are seeking to honor and serve him. He will help you more fully understand his Word and grasp his leading. Ask God to open your heart and mind to him. You have the promised hope of answered prayer.

7

Promised Refuge

God is our refuge and strength,
an ever-present help in trouble.
PSALM 46:1

Imagine you've gone out for an evening walk. The sky is cloudy but there's no rain. You walk for quite a while, enjoying the scenery. Then when you are a good distance from home, a sudden, violent storm blows up. Strong winds fling the trees around, rain pelts you, lightning streaks across the sky. It's scary! You need a safe place to hide from the storm. You need a refuge.

As storms blow up in your life (and they will), you will certainly hope for a refuge, a place where you can be safe from the danger of the storms. You do have the certain hope of a refuge in God. He is your safe place to hide from the storms of life. While you're tucked safely away he will refresh your strength so that when you must face those storms again, you'll be strong enough to be ready.

The beauty of his promised refuge and strength is that he is always available. He's always ready to help you. In fact, he's waiting for you to call out to him. Your hope for refuge and strength has been fulfilled!

8

Hope in What Jesus Says

That day when evening came, he said to his disciples, "Let us go over to the other side."

MARK 4:35

Jesus spent the day teaching. In the evening, he and his disciples got into a boat, and Jesus said, "Let us go over to the other side." It was a simple suggestion and probably not one his friends thought much about. But after they got out on the lake a sudden storm blew up. It was strong and the disciples were scared. But Jesus was sleeping. How could he sleep when they might die? You know the story—they woke him, he calmed the storm, then he asked why they had such little faith. Here's the thing . . . he said, "Let us go over to the other side." He didn't say, "Let's go halfway, then drown." The disciples didn't believe he meant what he said.

Do you believe Jesus will take care of you, guide you, and teach you? Do you believe what Scripture tells you about him, or do you question everything that happens to you? Do you only hope that he means what he says? Do you trust him to follow through and deliver you safely to the other side of whatever you're dealing with? Trust your hope in Jesus.

9

Jesus Cares

Jesus said to him, "Receive your sight; your faith has healed you." Immediately he received his sight and followed Jesus, praising God. When all the people saw it, they also praised God.

Jesus was on his way to Jericho. He was surrounded by people as usual. They followed him everywhere, some to see what he would do and some to benefit from his miracle power. It must have been a little chaotic around him as he walked down the road. In the noise of that moment a single voice cried out, "Jesus, have mercy on me!" (see v. 38). A blind man told Jesus that he wanted to see. With all the people pressing in around him, wanting things from him, Jesus heard that one voice . . . and he answered. He gave the blind man sight.

Jesus cares about any problem you have too. You can be certain in the hope that whatever you're dealing with, he cares, and he can handle it. Don't believe the lie that your problem is too insignificant for God to pay attention to. Don't believe the lie that you have disappointed him too often for him to help you this time. It's not true. You can be secure in the hope that he cares and he will help you get through whatever you're facing today.

10

Hope for the Future

"I know the plans I have for you," declares the LORD, "plans to prosper you and not to harm you, plans to give you hope and a future."

JEREMIAH 29:11

Did you have your life all planned out? You expected to do this thing by that date and that thing by the next date and on and on. But life doesn't always go by your plan, does it? You may not have been too far into your plan when things started shifting and changing. How did you handle those changes? Does your future look uncertain now? Would you still like to have things planned out so you know what to expect?

When situations and people start changing in your life, the future can look pretty confusing to you. But even if things look mysterious now, you can know that your future is all planned—by God. He may reveal it to you only one step at a time, but if you trust him, your hope can rest assured in his plan.

God's plans for you are always good, though they may not always be easy. If you're struggling with something right now, know that his plans include times of teaching you and growing you to become more like Jesus. Those lessons are learned through difficult times. Trust what he's doing in your life, and know that it is all for your good.

Hope for Better Times

I have told you these things, so that in me you may have peace. In this world you will have trouble. But take heart! I have overcome the world.

If you're a parent, you know that peace is a fleeting thing because a parent is often only as happy as her unhappiest child. If you're a citizen of the world—okay, that's everyone—then you know that peace in the world around you is an increasingly fleeting thing. It seems that people are more and more angry about more and more things. Peace between countries, people groups, families, and friends is very fragile. In these chaotic times is there any hope of peace?

Jesus warned his followers that life was going to get messy for them, and it did. It gets messy for you too. Broken relationships, health challenges, rebellious children—peace is hard to come by.

But Jesus doesn't leave you hopeless. You can have the hope of peace by putting your faith in him. He is in control and yes, life gets messy, but nothing surprises him. He is teaching you through the hard times to lean on him. That understanding can help you have peace for this day and, of course, you have the hope of heaven where peace will reign forever.

12

Hope for the Helpless

You, Lord, hear the desire of the afflicted;
you encourage them, and you listen to their cry.

Psalm 10:17

There are places around the world that seem to constantly be in a state of turmoil because of war, drought, storms, or poverty. Your heart must break for those people and the constant struggles they have to endure. It seems like they never have a chance to catch their breath or to have some peace and comfort in their world. It's hard to see where God might be in all of that.

There's no easy answer as to why God doesn't stop the wars or end the poverty or provide food and water. Why doesn't he help those people who are so afflicted? But you know that God is love, and his compassionate heart does care about them. The hope is that the people in those dire situations have comfort and peace in their hearts because they know that God has heard their cries.

The challenge is for Christians in more comfortable situations to reach out and help those in war-torn countries and poverty-stricken areas. Perhaps their help and hope is to come through God using your efforts.

13

Hope of Forgiveness

If we confess our sins, he is faithful and just and will forgive us our sins and purify us from all unrighteousness.

"I'm sorry. I'm so sorry. Please forgive me." When you want forgiveness from someone, you hope with all your heart that they will forgive your indiscretion and forget that it ever happened. That's the hope. But when someone asks your forgiveness, are you willing to forgive *and* forget? It's hard to forgive when you've been hurt, cheated, or lied to, isn't it?

That makes it even more amazing that when you ask God's forgiveness, he gives it, and not only does he forgive, he wipes away the memory of your sin. It's gone. There's no danger that he's keeping a list of your sins to bring up down the road somewhere. He isn't keeping a tally sheet to hit you with later. Whatever you have done, however you have sinned, no matter how many times or how often, God forgives you. Jesus paid the price for your sin, so when you confess your sin and ask his forgiveness, you get it! God promises his faithful forgiveness and cleansing for the rest of your life—all because he loves you. What a gift!

14

Hope for Growth

We boast in the hope of the glory of God. Not only so, but we also glory in our sufferings, because we know that suffering produces perseverance; perseverance, character; and character, hope.

ROMANS 5:2–4

What's the goal of exercise? It's to make you physically fit and therefore healthier, right? But exercise can be tiring and cause some pain. However, it's worth it in the long run because you get stronger, your balance is better, and your heart is healthier. You have to put in the work to get the benefit.

Spiritual growth also takes effort; some you can plan for, and some you cannot. Growing closer to God is something you want. Learning to trust him more—to trust his heart, to trust his plan—most often comes through difficulties in your life. When you're suffering or struggling and all you can do is hold on to him with all your strength, you learn.

The reward of holding on to God teaches you perseverance. Learning to keep on keeping on in your faith develops your character, which helps you become more like Christ in humility before God and dependence on him. This "spiritual workout" grows your faith-walk to make you more mature in Christ, and that's what God wants for you. Don't fight the process; instead, have hope in the outcome.

15

Hope for Guidance

Your word is a lamp for my feet,
a light on my path.

PSALM 119:105

Darkness so thick that you can't see your own hand in front of your face is pretty intense. Trying to make your way through such complete darkness is treacherous. You can trip over things, walk into things, and get completely disoriented so that you even go the wrong way.

Just a tiny little light in that complete darkness will shine like a beacon. It stands out brightly and gives you something to walk toward. It only takes a little bit of light to illuminate the darkness.

As you make your way through the chaos of life, do you sometimes feel that you're walking in total darkness? Do you long for some guidance and direction, some light in your world? God's Word will give you that. It becomes a light in your dark world, illuminating the path you should travel.

As you read God's Word and open your heart to its message and guidance, instructions for living in obedience to God become clearer. God's Word addresses how to obey him and how to treat other people. It lights your way and turns your heart toward obedience to God.

16

Hope in Your Advocate

I will ask the Father, and he will give you another advocate to help you and be with you forever—the Spirit of truth. The world cannot accept him, because it neither sees him nor knows him. But you know him, for he lives with you and will be in you.

John 14:16–17

When you, as a law-abiding citizen, have to plead your case to a police officer or worse, before a judge, it's scary. You might get so nervous that you can't say the words you need to speak to explain yourself or defend yourself. Even if you're innocent you start to get short of breath, and perspiration rolls down your forehead. What you need is an advocate—someone who can speak for you and make sense of the situation.

God knew you were going to need an advocate in all of life, so he gave you one—his Holy Spirit. Because of his Spirit you have the hope, or certainty, of being heard and understood.

The Holy Spirit pleads your case as necessary. He speaks to God on your behalf. He prays the prayers that are about things so intense you can't find words to pray about them. He resides in your heart and guides your understanding of Scripture. He maneuvers you through decisions and choices when you may not be sure what is right for you. The Holy Spirit is God's gift to you, and he offers all you need to learn about living for God and obeying him.

17

Hope for Knowledge

Call to me and I will answer you and tell you great and unsearchable things you do not know.

JEREMIAH 33:3

Clueless people sometimes act as though they know everything. They show an arrogance that's off-putting to others and disrespectful to God because they believe they have all the answers for their own lives and for others' lives. Humble people know they have very few answers, and the ones they do have are because God has revealed them.

Perhaps you feel that it would be nice to have a few more answers than you do have. Knowing what's ahead might make your today easier to take. Or facing the struggles in your life would be easier if you knew the why for them. God doesn't reveal everything about life to you, but he does promise to reveal things to you that you couldn't learn any other way. Ask him the questions rolling around in your mind.

Ask him to enlighten you on the meaning of Scripture. Ask him to help you understand the why of things in your life or in the world at large. Ask. He will reveal what he knows you can handle. The rest you must take through faith in his goodness and knowledge.

18

Hope for the End of Pain

God's dwelling place is now among the people, and he will dwell with them. They will be his people, and God himself will be with them and be their God. "He will wipe every tear from their eyes. There will be no more death" or mourning or crying or pain, for the old order of things has passed away.

REVELATION 21:3–4

There's a popular vacation spot that is referred to as "The Happiest Place on Earth," and it is definitely a fun place to go. Do you wish you could live permanently in a place that is perpetually happy? A place where you have no problems and nothing can make you sad? In a place like that, there would be no reason for sadness. Does that sound too good to be true? Well, it is if you're just talking about life here on earth. But the wonderful hope you have concerns heaven. God promises to bring you to heaven someday to live with him, and any pain and struggles you've experienced here on earth will be over. He promises there will be no tears in heaven, no death and no mourning; instead there will be joy and eternal life.

What a wonderful hope that is to hang on to. When life here is painful, remember that it's only for a time and that someday there will be no more pain and sorrow. You will have only the joy of being with Jesus in heaven!

19

Conqueror in Hope

No, in all these things we are more than conquerors through him who loved us. For I am convinced that neither death nor life, neither angels nor demons, neither the present nor the future, nor any powers, neither height nor depth, nor anything else in all creation, will be able to separate us from the love of God that is in Christ Jesus our Lord.

ROMANS 8:37–39

What an amazing promise! There is nothing in the world that can pull you away from God's love. Nothing and no one is strong enough or powerful enough to make that happen. The hope of God's permanent, assured, never-changing, always-present love is so sure that you can breathe a deep sigh of relief knowing his love is yours. His love is always surrounding, protecting, guiding, and comforting you.

There may be times when you feel you've failed God or when you deliberately walk away from him. There may be times when you wonder if he wants to be done with you because you've messed up too many times. But none of those situations will make him stop loving you.

No matter how many times Satan tries to discourage you and convince you that God is done with you, he's wrong. You are the winner, the conqueror over Satan, because God promises his love for you, forever and always. So take a deep breath, get up, and get on with life. Do better today than yesterday in obeying God and loving others. You are more than a conqueror—you are God's child!

Hope That God Hears

Lord my God, I called to you for help,
and you healed me.

If you have children you know that you learn to recognize their cries. When you hear your child cry out or call for you, you learn to recognize if the situation is urgent or if they're simply frustrated or perhaps angry. You base the quickness of your response on what you determine their need to be. Sometimes, if you perceive the need isn't urgent, your child may call out over and over until you finally respond. It's a mom thing, right?

When you call out to God for help, he hears you and he answers you. You have the assured hope that God is listening. He's paying attention and not basing the urgency of his answers on how desperate you sound.

Does he always do what you want at the very moment you want his action? No, he doesn't, because he knows what you need and when it's best for you to get it in order for your faith and dependence on him to grow deeper. But just as you care for your child's needs, God cares—even more— for yours. So even as he seems to delay his response, be assured that he is with you, listening to you, loving you, and holding you close.

21

Part of the Big Picture

My dear brothers and sisters, stand firm. Let nothing move you. Always give yourselves fully to the work of the Lord, because you know that your labor in the Lord is not in vain.

1 CORINTHIANS 15:58

It's encouraging to know that what you do makes a difference. You go to work and spend your mental and physical energy to do the job, and it's nice to know it's appreciated and that in some way it contributes to the bigger picture.

This is especially true of the work you do for God's kingdom. Satan will definitely try to discourage you. He will do his best to convince you that nothing you do is important or makes a difference. It can feel like you're just spinning your wheels and never getting anywhere.

But that's not true! Look at what this verse of Scripture tells you—*nothing* you do for God is done in vain. He will use every children's story you tell, every Sunday school lesson you teach, every kind word you speak in his name, every act of service you perform for someone else, every encouraging chat you share over coffee . . . everything you do for his kingdom will be used. You may not immediately see the effect of your service—it may be one piece of a puzzle that takes years to complete—but God tells you not to lose hope, because you *are* making a difference!

22

All You Need

I say to myself, "The LORD is my portion;
therefore I will wait for him."

LAMENTATIONS 3:24

o you sometimes think, "Well, if I had this or that thing, then I'd be fine," or "If this situation would happen or if this situation would change, then life would be better"?

Some folks live their whole lives looking for more of what they think they need instead of understanding that they have everything they really need in the Lord. In our society, accumulating more is seen as an important measure of success. Instead of being content with what they have and where they are, people keep pushing for God to do more or give them more. There is little satisfaction or contentment in their lives.

Have you come to the realization that God is all you need? Are you willing to wait for him to lead you to new places and new situations? Are you patiently waiting for him to give you what you need?

Your hope is in God, who, because of his deep love for you and his plan for your life, is truly all you need. He supplies your needs. He blesses you beyond anything you could hope for. Wait patiently for him to give you the "what's next" in your life.

Hope When All Seems Hopeless

While Jesus was still speaking, some people came from the house of Jairus, the synagogue leader. "Your daughter is dead," they said. "Why bother the teacher anymore?" Overhearing what they said, Jesus told him, "Don't be afraid; just believe."

MARK 5:35–36

Jairus knew his daughter was dying. That's why he went to ask Jesus for help. He knew Jesus could heal his girl, but before Jesus could do so, Jairus heard that his daughter was dead. He must have had a moment of hopelessness. Maybe he had just a moment of wondering why Jesus hadn't stopped his daughter's death. Did his faith shake just a little? If his heart had sunk, it must have bounced right back up when Jesus said, "Don't be afraid; just believe." Just like that, hope was born anew in Jairus's heart.

Maybe you've had a time when you were disappointed in God, a time when you prayed constantly for one specific situation and it felt like God didn't hear or at least didn't answer your prayer. It's hard sometimes to hold on, but faith is more than getting an immediate answer to your prayers. Faith is believing that Jesus will come through in his own good time because he knows what's best for you. So even when it is hard to wait and hard to believe, keep your hope strong in God because you know his character and his heart. Remember Jesus's words to Jairus. Faith is just believing.

24

A Life of Blessings

You make known to me the path of life;
you will fill me with joy in your presence,
with eternal pleasures at your right hand.

PSALM 16:11

Who doesn't want joy? Of course everyone does. The tension comes in trying to understand the difference between joy and happiness. Immediate pleasures bring temporary happiness, but true joy grows deep in your heart from the blessing of God's presence in your life. Joy comes from realizing that the Creator is guiding your life, that he wants to bless you and give you purpose, and that he promises eternity with him!

Hope based on God's presence and guidance in your life, as well as the blessing of being used for his work, gives great joy. God offers you the blessing of partnering with him in his work on earth—the joy of sharing his love with others and the privilege of being a part of their stories. There may be times when you make mistakes or wrong choices, but don't stress over them or over what the future holds. Learn from the past and keep moving forward. You can trust God, who holds your life in his hands. This true joy allows you the freedom to notice the many blessings God gives you—even the ordinary, everyday things that are gifts from him.

Life's Guidebook

> All Scripture is God-breathed and is useful for teaching, rebuking, correcting and training in righteousness, so that the servant of God may be thoroughly equipped for every good work.
>
> 2 Timothy 3:16–17

You do not need to have all the answers. Is that a relief or what? In fact, it's virtually impossible for you to have the answers for all the situations you face in life. What you need is wisdom that comes from a greater source than your own mind. This comes as no surprise to God; that's why you have the Bible at your disposal. God's wisdom for anything you need to know is contained in Scripture.

Scripture answers any questions you may have about obeying God and what it means to be submitted to him so that your life is focused only on serving him. Scripture teaches you how to live in community with others, loving and serving them as God would have you do. God guides you through specific situations in life by making his Word come alive to you at just the right moment to answer a question you are struggling with. When you read God's Word with a submitted heart, he shows you when you are doing things that do not honor him.

God's Word prepares you for a life of service to him by helping you come to know him better. Everything you need to know is in his Word.

26

Hope in a New Attitude

We are God's handiwork, created in Christ Jesus to do good works, which God prepared in advance for us to do.

EPHESIANS 2:10

What's your crabby quotient? Do you start off each day with a chip on your shoulder? What causes it? Feeling unappreciated? Too much work? Not enjoying your work? Feeling like you just don't matter ... even to God? Whoa. Stop right there. You matter to God in bigger ways than you can imagine.

What does the word *handiwork* conjure up in your mind? Perhaps you think of creative work done by hand, such as knitting or crocheting. Maybe it's the talents of someone who paints lovely pictures, sews, or builds things. Almost certainly handiwork is something made by hand, which means the creator of that piece has put time and energy into making it. Each piece of handiwork is special to its creator because it is work from the heart, and the creator has a personal investment in it.

Here's where the "you matter to God" comes into play. You are his handiwork. He made you with a special job in mind through which you can serve him, and he's already equipped you to do that job. You are special to him because he made you. He equipped you. He has something special for you to do. So keep your crabby attitude at bay, and serve God in joy.

27

Growing Older and Wiser

Teach us to number our days,
that we may gain a heart of wisdom.
PSALM 90:12

How do you feel about growing older? Are you dropping bundles of money on creams that promise to slow down the look of aging? Or hair coloring to push away the gray? Do you fight the middle-age bulge to keep your youthful figure? It's a lot of work and expense to try to appear youthful when you're not.

Of course it's a good thing to take care of yourself so you stay as healthy as possible into your mature years. But instead of focusing only on staying young, perhaps it's better to embrace aging and appreciate the wisdom you've gained from living as long as you have. Take hope in that wisdom so you can share it with the young people in your life and save them from having to learn some things the hard way. The wisdom you've gained in life teaches you to become a better person, to focus on what really matters, to not sweat the small stuff, to make God your priority, and to treat people with kindness and respect. The wisdom gained through the experience of living life makes your golden years all the more golden. Start as young as you can to gain wisdom with each year of living.

28

Hope in a Strong Finish

*Being confident of this, that he who began a good work in you
will carry it on to completion until the day of Christ Jesus.*

PHILIPPIANS 1:6

The older you get, the faster the years fly by, right? In the
blink of an eye your toddler is in high school or you're
a decade older or a "young" friend is retiring. Like most
folks you probably have things on your radar that you plan
to do someday. Not just vacations or home improvements
but things that are service or ministry focused, things you
feel will really matter in the big scheme of life and to God's
kingdom. Then one day you glance at the calendar and realize that time has been flying by and you have not done any
of those things. That's discouraging, isn't it?

Well, here's a solid hope for you—God isn't finished with
you yet! He knows how quickly the years are passing. He's
paying attention and, without a doubt, he is using you to bless
others in ways you may not even recognize. The wonderful

thing about serving God is that sometimes you are intentional in what you do, and he has specific work for you, but even when you aren't intentional, he still uses your talents and gifts to bless others and to share his love. One thing you'll never retire from is serving God!

29

Hope for the Growth of the Kingdom

This is what the kingdom of God is like. A man scatters seed on the ground. Night and day, whether he sleeps or gets up, the seed sprouts and grows, though he does not know how.

MARK 4:26–27

It sometimes feels like the evil one is winning. When you hear the news of wars and hatred around the world, it's frightening. Even more discouraging are the reports of evil done one-on-one when people are assaulted or murdered. Why isn't the message of God's love stopping people from such wickedness?

You also hear of Christians being persecuted around the world and forced into secrecy. Why doesn't God prevent that?

The hope you must grab on to is that God's kingdom is actually growing. It may be slow. It may be under the radar.

But nothing done for God is wasted. Hearts are changed and challenged. Even in places around the world where the church is forced underground, believers' faith is growing stronger. God will not be defeated!

Don't be discouraged. Keep hope! Stay strong in your faith, living for Christ. Stay strong in praying for Christians around the world and in giving to ministries that are making a difference. Stay strong in praying against the evil that people do to one another. Stay strong in your own service to God. God's kingdom will survive and prosper!

30

Hope of Purpose

Therefore we do not lose heart. Though outwardly we are wasting away, yet inwardly we are being renewed day by day. For our light and momentary troubles are achieving for us an eternal glory that far outweighs them all. So we fix our eyes not on what is seen, but on what is unseen, since what is seen is temporary, but what is unseen is eternal.

2 CORINTHIANS 4:16–18

Perhaps you aren't at the stage of life where you feel that you're physically or mentally wasting away. If you do feel somewhat that way, then hopefully you'll have a reenergizing phase. As time passes and you see yourself changing, it's tempting to think that you no longer have much purpose. But regardless of what's happening to your body, God still has a plan for the rest of your life.

Don't just focus on what your body can't do anymore. Whatever is going on with it is only a part of who you are. Sure, there are things you can't do right now, but God says there are more important things happening. Your eternal glory is still being developed. Work on your attitude by asking God to show you what your purpose is for him this day. Don't let physical limitations discourage you. Keep your heart focused on Jesus because what he's teaching you is what's most important. He still has a purpose for your life. It may be different than it was before, but it's just as important!

31

Hope through No Prejudice

Do not forget to show hospitality to strangers, for by so doing some people have shown hospitality to angels without knowing it.

Hebrews 13:2

Be kind. Just be kind. It shouldn't be that hard, but for some people it seems to be. They find it difficult to be kind and gracious to anyone who is even a little different from them. That's too bad because they may be missing a huge blessing by being so standoffish.

If you knew that the homeless person asking for a handout was an angel, wouldn't you hand them a twenty-dollar bill? If someone from another country and another religion needed a question answered about living in this country, and if you knew that person was an angel, you'd kindly speak to them and give answers, right?

You see, that's the thing. Your prejudices against certain groups of people may be hurting you more than they hurt them. Show the love of Christ to *all* you come in contact with. You may bless an angel, and you will definitely show love that is reflective of God's love. If you happen to help another person, well that's good too, because you will be blessed in the process!

32

Firewall of Hope

You, LORD, are a shield around me,
my glory, the One who lifts my head high.
PSALM 3:3

Websites are protected by firewalls. A firewall is sort of like a shield. It determines who can and can't get through to the website based on predetermined security rules. Protection is important.

It's nice to know you have protection when you need it— and you do have it! If you've asked Jesus to be your Savior, his Holy Spirit has come into your heart, and he is with you constantly. He never leaves you. The Holy Spirit protects your heart, which is the core of your being. The condition of your heart affects your thoughts and actions. So the Bible tells you to guard your heart because it's so important to your mental and spiritual well-being. The Holy Spirit is a holy firewall around your heart.

More than that, God is the shield around you. He watches out for you. He protects you more times each day than you can probably even imagine. Nothing happens to you without God's knowledge. He is your shield against the world and against Satan's efforts to harm you or pull you away from God. Depend on God. Talk to him. Tell him what you need and go forward with courage knowing that he is protecting you!

33

Hope in Being Heard

This is the confidence we have in approaching God: that if we ask anything according to his will, he hears us. And if we know that he hears us—whatever we ask—we know that we have what we asked of him.

1 JOHN 5:14–15

I t means a lot when you feel that you are being heard. When you have a conversation with some people they appear to be preoccupied, busy with their phone, or just not paying attention to you. So when you engage in conversation with someone who gives you their full attention and cares about what you say, you feel heard and valued as a person.

It's something to have another person value you enough to listen to you, but it's even more amazing when you realize that God himself listens when you speak to him. He gives you his complete attention. He wants to hear what you have to say to him.

Even more wonderful is that if you stay close to God so that your heart is submitted to him, then you trust his plans for you, so as you pray, you're asking him to do what he really wants to do. Be assured that he will not only hear your prayers but answer them and guide every step you take.

Thank God for listening to your prayers. Thank him for caring enough to hear you.

34

Hope in Closeness

Come near to God and he will come near to you.

JAMES 4:8

There's comfort in being close to someone you love. Hopefully as a child you had the opportunity to snuggle close to someone as they read a book to you. Or perhaps you've been the adult reader with a child or grandchild squeezed in close. There's comfort in a hug from someone you love when you need encouragement. There's also comfort in just sitting with someone—no words needed—just being near someone who you know cares about you.

When you need comfort or encouragement, draw near to God. Go to a quiet place alone and meditate on his love for you. Give yourself time to put aside all the things clamoring for your attention and care. Push those things aside and think about God and his love for you. Choose a Bible verse about his care for you that's especially meaningful to you, and really think about it. When you come near to him, he meets you there. He promised he would. There is no greater hope for comfort than to know that you are in God's presence and that he loves you completely and unconditionally. Be still with him. Let his love flow over you.

35

Hope in Secret Giving

When you give to the needy, do not let your left hand know what your right hand is doing, so that your giving may be in secret. Then your Father, who sees what is done in secret, will reward you.

MATTHEW 6:3–4

Secret blessings are such a joy! If you've ever been the recipient of an anonymous gift, you know how wonderful it feels to know that someone cares enough to give you a gift. It means that the giver is paying attention to you—to what you need or to what you like. It also means that the giver is not giving the gift in order to be thanked or to receive praise for their generosity. The giver just wants to bless you.

Are you a secret gift-giver? Giving in secret without hoping for recognition or praise is truly sacrificial giving. When you give completely from the goodness of your heart, God will reward that generosity. His reward will probably not be a monetary reward, but whatever it is, it will include the joyous blessing of knowing you have helped another person in some way.

So don't give to the needy just for the tax break. Don't give so that you get a pat on the back. Don't give expecting anything in return. Give from a heart that is grateful for the blessings you have, and hope for a "well done" from the Lord when you meet him in heaven.

36

Hope in God's GPS

*I have hidden your word in my heart
that I might not sin against you.*

PSALM 119:11

You need to get from Point A to Point B. There are several possible routes, but how do you know which one is best? You could drive around trying various routes, getting lost, taking hours of time, using lots of gas, and possibly giving up in frustration and never reaching your destination. Or you could grab a map and outline the streets to take from Point A to Point B. Maybe you could plug the addresses into your GPS and let its gentle voice tell you, "Drive straight. Turn left. You have arrived at your destination."

If only life were that simple. If only there were a map or GPS to guide your choices, behaviors, attitudes, and actions. There is! It's called the Bible. It is your map, your GPS for guiding you in how to be successful in living for God. Reading the stories in it helps you to learn God's character and shows you how he interacts with his people. His Word gives you guidelines for honoring, obeying, and worshiping him and for living in community with others. It challenges you to love others and honor them with your service.

God's desire is that you will memorize verses from his Word so that its wisdom is readily available to you for whatever challenges life brings. God's Word is your guide and your comfort all at the same time!

37

Blessed Hope

The grace of God has appeared that offers salvation to all people. It teaches us to say "No" to ungodliness and worldly passions, and to live self-controlled, upright and godly lives in this present age, while we wait for the blessed hope—the appearing of the glory of our great God and Savior, Jesus Christ.

TITUS 2:11–13

The blessed hope of Jesus's return to take you to heaven— what a glorious thing to anticipate! Do you spend your days standing, looking heavenward while believing that Jesus might come back at any moment? Probably not, because of, well . . . life. But you should live with that anticipation always in your mind so that it flavors all you do and every choice you make.

How you live in the here and now reflects what you truly believe about the blessed hope of Jesus's return. That's a sobering thought, isn't it? It's true though, because if you believe that Jesus could return at any moment, then you will be careful how you live. You will choose to turn away from actions and choices that do not honor God. The things the world offers you as fun or rewarding but that do not align with living for God will not be so tempting. You will choose to honor God and to love others as he instructed. You will be self-controlled about serving and obeying him because the most important thing is to be guiltless when Jesus returns. That truly will make his return a blessed hope!

38

Reflecting Jesus's Love

May the God who gives endurance and encouragement give you the same attitude of mind toward each other that Christ Jesus had, so that with one mind and one voice you may glorify the God and Father of our Lord Jesus Christ.

ROMANS 15:5–6

Do you play nice with others? If not, why not? Okay, some people are more of a challenge to love than others. Some people choose to be critical and judgmental, which makes them no fun to be around. Their negative attitudes may seep into your own behavior, too, and you certainly don't want that.

If there are people you have difficulty treating in the same way Jesus did, ask God for help. How did Jesus treat others? He was kind to those who were struggling, helping them as only he could. He gave to them. He spent time with them. Of course, he also held accountable those who needed to be held accountable.

For those you have trouble being kind to, ask Jesus for his help and strength to be kind. Ask him to help you see the good in those people and to be able to concentrate on that.

Make it your goal to reflect Jesus to all with whom you come in contact. Yes, at times you'll need his help to be patient and kind. But you will be glorifying God and sharing his love through your behavior.

39

Hope of a Clean Slate

Repent, then, and turn to God, so that your sins may be wiped out, that times of refreshing may come from the Lord.

ACTS 3:19

Whew. Have there been times when you just wanted to start over? Maybe a day has gotten off to a bad start, and you just want to start anew. Or maybe you've really messed up in a friendship and you want a do-over. Of course, in all that starting over you want your mistakes and wrongs to be totally forgotten. Otherwise it wouldn't be a clean slate. However, wiping the slate clean is a hard thing for people to do. They may be okay with forgiving the ways you've hurt them, but forgetting? Well, that's a different story.

The human reticence to forget being wronged makes God's ability to forgive *and* forget even more of a blessing. You have the hope of a clean slate with God, time after time after time! When you repent—turn away from your sin—he forgives and forgets. He wipes out the sin and the *memory* of the sin. What a blessing! This is God's love in action. When you repent of your sin, he wants to believe the best of you, and he gives you the opportunity to move forward with a clean slate.

40

Don't Be Afraid

> *Have I not commanded you? Be strong and courageous. Do not be afraid; do not be discouraged, for the LORD your God will be with you wherever you go.*
>
> JOSHUA 1:9

What scares you? What makes you weak in the knees and afraid to face a new day? Maybe you're afraid of failure in a difficult job or even in a relationship. Maybe you're afraid of a partner or of someone who is bullying you or stalking you. Maybe you're afraid of disappointing God.

You're told over and over in Scripture not to be afraid . . . *fear not . . . be courageous . . . be strong.* So, why is it so hard? God promises over and over to be with you and that he will never leave you. He is protecting you, guiding you, strengthening you. Why is life still frightening?

The bottom line is that, for whatever reason, it just is sometimes. But each time you need to be strong, read the verses that promise you God's presence and strength. Be reminded that you are never, ever alone. There is no actual reason to be afraid or discouraged, because God, who is more powerful than anything or anyone, is with you, fighting for you, guarding you, loving you. Stay focused on him!

41

A Humble Heart

When you pray, go into your room, close the door and pray to your Father, who is unseen. Then your Father, who sees what is done in secret, will reward you.

MATTHEW 6:6

God values a humble follower and judges a person who functions on pride. Some Christians make a big show of their Christianity, but their hearts aren't submitted to God. They live with pride in themselves and are judgmental and critical of others. Often they're more concerned with what others think of them than with what God thinks.

To have hope in pleasing God, submit your heart to him and be humble. Don't make a show of your relationship with him; in fact, God says to do your serious personal prayer time in private. Of course praying with others is a good thing too. But when you're pouring out the secrets in your heart, keep it between you and God. The intense personal conversations you have with him will grow your faith and trust in him. The goal of your prayer life is to share the depths of your soul with him. That's something that should be done in private, not as a show before others. God will hear the desires of your humble heart, and he will reward your trust in him.

42

A Servant's Heart

The LORD is my shepherd, I lack nothing.
PSALM 23:1

There's a song in the well-loved musical *Fiddler on the Roof* about Tevye's dream of being a wealthy man. One line in that song asks this question: "Would it spoil some vast eternal plan if I were a wealthy man?"* Maybe you ask that, too, as the financial stresses of life weigh down on you. How does God decide who should be blessed with material comforts while others have to struggle to make ends meet?

Perhaps God isn't concerned with how much money you have. His focus is on giving you what you need so that you can become more like Jesus. What does that mean? It means he gives you a servant's heart and a selfless compassion for others. As a Christ follower, you humbly submit to God's will for your life because you trust him completely, and you love

*Jerry Bock and Sheldon Harnick, "If I Were a Rich Man," *Fiddler on the Roof*, ©1964.

others—even those who are different from you—as much as you love yourself.

The wonderful thing is that God guides and leads you through this growth journey because of his love for you. You have the hope of becoming more like Jesus because God gives you everything you need for the process.

43

No Half-Hearted Searching

You will seek me and find me when you seek me with all your heart.

JEREMIAH 29:13

$\mathcal{A}$ half-hearted commitment to Jesus simply will not work. Scripture tells you that God won't share your heart with any other thing or person; he must be Number One in your heart. Loving and serving God will only enhance your life and make all other things in your life even more wonderful.

Do you hope to know God more deeply and honestly? That happens by submitting to him and asking him to push all other things aside so that he is most important to you. That is a moment-by-moment process as personal priorities keep pushing their way back into your focus. Your submission will be repeated over and over as Satan continuously pushes other things ahead of God, trying to pull you away from serving him.

The wonderful hope you have is that as you submit to God and allow him to rule in your heart, you will be blessed to know him more and more deeply. He loves you very much, and fully loving him will be an amazing blessing to you.

44

Hope in Another's Prayers

Confess your sins to each other and pray for each other so that you may be healed. The prayer of a righteous person is powerful and effective.

James 5:16

$\mathcal{A}$re you supposed to confess your sins to anyone who will listen? Should it be a public broadcast? Of course not. God wants you to live in community with other believers. You need to hold one another accountable in your Christian walk and to encourage one another in your faith. A group of friends with whom you have an intimate spiritual relationship is the place where you can share your failings as well as your victories and the lessons you're learning.

One of the blessings of living in community with other believers is the privilege of praying for one another. When you confess your sins, your friends commit to praying for you and helping you to overcome those sins, and you can do the same for them. In that way you become a part of one another's Christian walk so your bonds of unity go even deeper.

God promises to hear the prayers of his children. He also says that the prayers of those who are seeking to know him in a deep and meaningful way and who love one another with a humble, sincere love will get results. Your prayers are powerfully strong in getting things done!

45

Hope in the Stillness

Be still, and know that I am God;
I will be exalted among the nations,
I will be exalted in the earth.

As a believer, do you hope for God's kingdom to grow so that more and more people will know him? Of course you do. Do you know your role in making that happen? You have one. God gives every believer a job to do. One way of helping the message of God's love spread around the world is something so simple that perhaps you've never thought about its importance . . . be still.

In the chaos of the world you live in, there are constantly voices shouting information at you or demanding your attention and your allegiance. It's hard to think with all the noise, and it's hard to know which voices to listen to and which ones speak truth. God says to be quiet and wait for his voice to stand out. Then you'll know which voice to follow. As your heart turns to God in the quietness, you will be amazed at his greatness, power, and love. That amazement will be hard to keep to yourself, so you will likely want to share your love for God with others. That's how your stillness plays a role in telling the world about God.

46

Hope in Weakness

My grace is sufficient for you, for my power is made perfect in weakness.

2 Corinthians 12:9

This verse seems like an oxymoron, doesn't it? The idea that your weakness makes God's power perfect seems strange. But when you realize that your weakness provides the opportunity for God's power to shine, then it makes sense.

When you try to power through life in your own strength, God doesn't get credit for the things that are happening. You may say that you need him and trust him, but your devotion is not evident by your actions. When others see your pride in your own abilities, they know that God is not the source of your power.

But when you admit your weaknesses and your need for God to take over your heart, then by his grace . . . he does. His power becomes your power. His strength becomes your strength. By your words, actions, and heart devotion, God receives the credit for your strength in overcoming weakness. He gets the praise for healing your heart wounds. His strength is what enables you to do his work. God loving others through you is apparent to all around you, and his power is perfected by your weakness because you acknowledge your need for him.

47

Over-the-Top Power

Now to him who is able to do immeasurably more than all we ask or imagine, according to his power that is at work within us, to him be glory in the church and in Christ Jesus throughout all generations, for ever and ever! Amen.

Ephesians 3:20–21

When you were a child, did you make a wish list for birthday or Christmas gifts? Those lists are usually filled with anything you can think of—over-the-top big gifts (after all, it is a *wish* list) and practical, more affordable gifts. You probably didn't have much hope of receiving the over-the-top big gift, but it never hurt to try. After all, Grandma might come through.

There is one time when you will receive more than you ask for, more than you ever expect to get. God is the over-the-top gift giver. His unlimited power works in your heart to make you more like Jesus—loving, humble, and obedient to God. His power in your life makes things possible that you never even dared to dream, and it gives you unimaginable courage and strength.

Whatever God does in your life is to glorify himself for all to see. When you submit to his power, you have the blessing of playing a part in his kingdom being grown throughout the world!

48

Hope in Grace-Filled Speech

Let your conversation be always full of grace, seasoned with salt, so that you may know how to answer everyone.

COLOSSIANS 4:6

The Bible often mentions the power of words. What you say to others and how you speak—the tone and attitude of your words—matter. This verse tells you to make sure your words are full of grace. What does it mean to speak words of grace? It hearkens back to "Do unto others as you would have them do unto you," doesn't it? Speak words of kindness, lifting others up and reinforcing all that is good in them. Compliment jobs well done and efforts made. Encourage others to try new things, challenging them to keep on going when things get tough.

Your grace-filled conversation should be comforting, filled with compassion for what those around you are going through. Your love, which reflects God's love, begins with what and how you speak to others; from there, let your actions reinforce your words.

Salt-seasoned words of grace are encouraging, challenging, loving words that share the truth of God's love and draw others to him. They reflect your relationship with Jesus and how you value other people. Be careful about the words you speak. Your words have power, so use your power for good by speaking kindly.

49

Life Dreams

> "My thoughts are not your thoughts,
>   neither are your ways my ways," declares
>   the LORD.
> "As the heavens are higher than the earth,
>   so are my ways higher than your ways
>   and my thoughts than your thoughts."
>
> ISAIAH 55:8–9

It's good to have a dream for your future life—a dream career, a dream marriage, dream children, a dream retirement. Of course everyone dreams of the best life, and there is nothing wrong with that. But your well-laid plans will probably not go as you hope. Plans seldom do.

What's your response when you realize that what you expected your life to be is never going to happen? Instead of getting upset, think about it this way: God has a much better plan for your life than you do. After all, God knows the expanse of your whole life—people you will meet, choices you will make, careers you will have, family you will have. He knows how all those things will play into making you the person you become. He knows the plans he has for you and the ways you will be a part of others' lives.

Embrace his plan for your life and celebrate with hope that his plan is better, more exciting, and more fulfilling than even your best dream ever could have been!

50

Hope in Silence

Even fools are thought wise if they keep silent,
and discerning if they hold their tongues.

PROVERBS 17:28

Do you hope that other people think you're wise? Would you like to be a person other people come to for advice? There's a simple way to appear wise, even as you're gaining the wisdom that comes with age, and that is to keep quiet. Easier said than done for some folks, right? But the fact is that sometimes when you spout out opinions or advice without being asked or without having the full story, you appear foolish.

But keeping quiet and listening to what others say makes you appear wise. It also shows that you are interested in other people and their opinions. You are willing to listen to them and hear their stories. You care what situations they are dealing with.

While you are keeping quiet, spend time in Scripture and seek God's wisdom for life. Be careful to listen to his Spirit instructing and guiding you as to when to speak and how to present your comments. Share God's wisdom . . . not yours.

51

Hope for Contentment

Keep your lives free from the love of money and be content with what you have, because God has said,

> *"Never will I leave you;*
> *never will I forsake you."*

HEBREWS 13:5

No matter how much money a person has, it never seems to be enough. The goal is to get more. The love of money becomes an addiction so that time and effort is focused on having more of it. It puts your priority on work over time with family, friends, and even God.

Why is money so important? Why is there never enough? Why is it so hard to be content? Our culture screams that you need more, more, more, which makes it very hard to be content with just having enough for what you need. Those always striving for more are seldom content.

Contentment is being happy with what God gives you. It means you are satisfied with having enough to meet your needs and with sharing any excess with those who don't have enough. Sometimes you even make do with less and share from funds you actually need in order to help someone else. Being content allows you to give others hope through your generosity.

52

Hope from Living Water

Jesus answered, "Everyone who drinks this water will be thirsty again, but whoever drinks the water I give them will never thirst. Indeed, the water I give them will become in them a spring of water welling up to eternal life."

JOHN 4:13–14

Jesus warned against drinking the water of deception. What was he talking about? He was warning against putting your faith in anything or anyone other than him. Some people get sucked into believing whatever the popular thoughts are, whether they honor God or not. Those popular ideas come and go, so it's hard to build a life on them.

The hope for true joy and contentment is found only in believing that Jesus is God's Son who came to earth to live as a human being and to die for your sins. He rose again, and his Holy Spirit lives in your heart to teach and guide you to obey God and live for him. That belief is the water you can drink that will give you the hope of eternal life and contentment deep in your heart. That contentment grows and deepens as your understanding of him grows. Since he never changes, you can count on him for the rest of your life. Just as Jesus said, giving your heart to him and believing in Scripture becomes a bubbling well of life in your heart.

53

Hope in God's Power

The LORD is the great God,
   the great King above all gods.
In his hand are the depths of the earth,
   and the mountain peaks belong to him.
The sea is his, for he made it,
   and his hands formed the dry land.

PSALM 95:3–5

Are you fascinated by creation? What part of God's creation speaks most clearly to you of his creative power? Is it the majestic rugged mountains that seem to reach to the heavens or the massive oceans with crashing waves? Maybe it's the flat prairies with waves of grasses and grains gently blowing, or giant sequoia trees or meandering brooks. Do you look at impressive thunderstorms with flashing lightning or at stars shooting across the night sky and immediately marvel at God's creativity and awesome power?

The very first verse in the Bible gives God the credit for everything in our world, even in the universe. It was all made by his hand and came from his great mind. All creation speaks of his mighty power, from storms, volcanoes, and earthquakes to tiny hummingbirds and gentle butterflies. His power controls all of these. Just a word from him and the sun stands still, a storm stops, a river divides, or a bush burns.

That amazing power is where you put your hope because it is the power of *your* Creator . . . God, who loves you!

54

Hope of Loving a Difficult Person

We love because he first loved us.
1 JOHN 4:19

Aarrgghh! Have you ever wanted to just walk away from a person and cut her out of your life? A friend— or family member—who knows just how to push your buttons and totally frustrate you can make life unpleasant. Maybe she knows how annoying she is, and she does it on purpose just to get a reaction from you. Ugh. No fun. So you take the high road and just push her out of your daily life, avoiding her as much as possible. How are you supposed to love someone who is basically unlovable?

There is only one hope for being able to love someone like that: God. It *is* possible to love a difficult person by allowing God's love to flow through you. Think about it . . . you aren't always lovable, but God constantly loves you. Sometimes you deliberately disobey God, but he doesn't stop loving you. His example of love is constant, steady, forgiving, and selfless. You can have the hope of loving a difficult person by asking God to love through you over and over until one day you realize that you do, in fact, actually love that person!

55

Hope of Family

See what great love the Father has lavished on us, that we should be called children of God! And that is what we are!

1 JOHN 3:1

Our families can be wonderful or flawed and usually are a mix of both. Our times together can include laughter or tears, good advice or bad examples, but one thing is for sure—we know who's family and who's not. We know where we belong and who our tribe is.

When you accept Christ as your Savior, you are adopted into God's family. You are a child of the King, and being a member of his family is amazing! Your heavenly Father loves you even more than your earthly family does, and he is happy to call you his child. As you learn more and more about him you will see the evidence of his DNA in your heart. The familial characteristics will be obvious in the way you love others in humility and self-denial.

Whatever your earthly family is like, you belong to the family of God.

Celebrate your position in his family by learning about your Father and how you can reflect his DNA to those around you.

56

Clothed in Love

Therefore, as God's chosen people, holy and dearly loved, clothe yourselves with compassion, kindness, humility, gentleness and patience. Bear with each other and forgive one another if any of you has a grievance against someone. Forgive as the Lord forgave you. And over all these virtues put on love, which binds them all together in perfect unity.

COLOSSIANS 3:12–14

I t shouldn't be hard to be nice, should it? You are a child of God. His DNA is flowing through your veins and one of his major characteristics is love. How can you love others the way that God does? How can you even hope to love that well? God lists the characteristics of his love in these verses. None of them are really difficult. To clothe yourself with these characteristics means you have to intentionally put them on just as you put on the pieces of your physical clothing each day.

Treat those around you with compassion, which means showing you care about the struggles they face. Be kind in the way you treat others, especially the way you speak to them. Be humble and lift others up. Be gentle in all you say and do. Be patient with those who don't do things the way you would do them. Bear with them in their mistakes and the learning process as they are maturing. Forgive when you must and, more than anything else, love others. Just love. When you do these things, you have the hope of being united with others by your love for Christ.

57

All In

Trust in the Lord with all your heart
and lean not on your own understanding;
in all your ways submit to him,
and he will make your paths straight.

When you are part of a team or club, it is expected that your loyalty and support will be to that group. It's not really a good idea to try to split your support between your team and a competitor. You can't fully support both of them. You're either all in or you're not in at all.

Your relationship with God is an all-in or not-in-at-all kind of thing too. God doesn't want you to sort of trust him; he wants all your trust—about everything—from deep in your whole heart because you know that God is the only and best way. No one else you trust has your best interest in mind. You can't even trust yourself more than you trust him. He has a better understanding of the world, your life, and his work than you do. So trust him enough to submit to him. That means you let him have control of your life, and you don't resist his guidance or plan. You have to fully trust him in order to do that. When you're all in for God, your heart belongs to him and your trust is in him. He will guide and direct your life.

58

Hope for Rescue

Be strong, do not fear;
your God will come,
*   he will come with vengeance;*
with divine retribution
*   he will come to save you.*

Numerous times Scripture tells you to "fear not." Just don't be afraid. But the reality is that you will run into some pretty stress-inducing situations in life, and some of them can be overwhelming. When your heart is afraid, your trust in God is tested. That's when you know how deep your trust is and whether you really believe he has your back. Times of testing offer times of growth. If God rescues you when there is nothing frightening happening, it doesn't seem like such a big deal. But when you're scared or things look hopeless and you see God show up to save you—even push your enemies away from you—then you know that he's taking care of you. You know you can trust him.

The more often you see God rescue you, the easier it will be to trust him more deeply. Step out in faith and trust him with whatever you are facing today. See his protection, and then the next time you're afraid, trust will come a bit easier. Trust is a growth process, and the reward is no fear!

59

Hope in God's Nearness

The Lord is near to all who call on him,
to all who call on him in truth.

PSALM 145:18

A large crowded room, like an auditorium or a stadium, is a cacophony of noise. Voices shouting to be heard above the roar make it hard to have a conversation at all. If you should happen to get separated from the ones you came with, it may take awhile to find them again. You might notice your friend through the crowd of people and call out to her, even shout to get her attention so you can reunite with her. But with all the people and noise, she can't hear you and doesn't even see you. Getting back together is going to be a challenge.

That will never happen with God. He promises that when you call out to him, he will come right to you, as close as possible. His closeness means he is protecting, guiding, and loving you.

It is a wonderful hope that God is always available to you. He loves you so much, and he wants to be close to you. He's actually happy when you call to him, so call to him daily and believe that he will come.

60

Stay Alert!

Be alert and of sober mind. Your enemy the devil prowls around like a roaring lion looking for someone to devour. Resist him, standing firm in the faith, because you know that the family of believers throughout the world is undergoing the same kind of sufferings.

1 PETER 5:8–9

$\mathcal{P}$ay attention! Don't let your guard down. Don't ever let yourself get too comfortable, feeling like you've got a handle on this faith stuff. That lack of focus is just what Satan is watching for. He's always looking for a chink in your armor where he can sneak in and do his work of pulling you away from God. His hunger to do that is never satisfied. He wants to pull more and more believers away from their faith in God.

Don't let Satan win! Stand firm by staying connected to Jesus. Read his Word. Don't just read it; meditate on it, learn it, and let it sink deep into your heart so that you can gain strength by pulling its words up in your memory when you feel tempted or hopeless. Quoting Scripture is one major way you defeat the devil. He has no response to it.

Take comfort in the fact that you aren't the only person Satan is after. Every believer in the whole world has to fight a battle against him. Stay alert and serious about your relationship with God.

61

Lavished with Blessings

In him we have redemption through his blood, the forgiveness of sins, in accordance with the riches of God's grace that he lavished on us.

EPHESIANS 1:7–8

You are redeemed because Jesus died on the cross. What does *redeemed* mean? It means your sins have been compensated for . . . the price has been paid by Jesus's shed blood on the cross. Because you are redeemed, your sins are forgiven. There are no penalties you need to pay. It's pretty awesome that your sins won't come back to haunt you somewhere down the road. By God's grace they are gone . . . forever forgotten. God has taken care of everything for you. He has made you a member of his family and blesses you abundantly every day.

There's a beautiful word in these verses . . . *lavished*. You see, God didn't just give you the basics of what you need or offer the very minimum of blessings. No, he turned the blessings jar upside down and poured them out. He blessed you with his grace more than you could have dreamed, more than you ever expected, more than you could imagine. He loves you so much that he just wants to give you more and more blessings, grace, and love.

62

True Love

I love those who love me,
and those who seek me find me.
PROVERBS 8:17

It's a beautiful thing to be in love. When you are newly in love you want to be with the one who is the object of your affection all the time. You long to hear what your love is thinking, what he likes to do, where he likes to go, what food he likes to eat. You want to know everything about him. You never get enough! It's wonderful.

Do you love God like that? Do you long to spend time with him? Do you want to know everything about him? Do you read his Word to learn his character and his likes and dislikes? It's all there for you. Just as spending time with your loved one is the best way to get to know him, the only way to get to know God is to spend time with him. The beauty of reaching out to get to know God is that he eagerly meets you, and he loves you even more than you love him! The hope of loving God is the certainty that he loves you. There is no unrequited love with him! He promises that when you look for him, you will find him. God wants to be with you!

63

Hoping for What You Don't Have Yet

We ourselves, who have the firstfruits of the Spirit, groan inwardly as we wait eagerly for our adoption to sonship, the redemption of our bodies. For in this hope we were saved. But hope that is seen is no hope at all. Who hopes for what they already have?

ROMANS 8:23–24

Being a Christian and learning to know God better means that you long to do better in your efforts to live for him. You long to obey him more consistently. You long to love the way he loves—to love him and to love others. Your mind knows that on this earth you will never achieve the perfection you hope for. But you have the hope of Jesus coming back to take you to heaven. When you get to heaven you will no longer sin. You will no longer struggle with staying close to

God or with moving forward in the process of becoming more like Jesus. You will have everything you have hoped for.

You have to wait for the reward of heaven, and you have no clue as to when it will come. So you wait. Waiting isn't easy, is it? You hope for heaven, but you don't have it yet; if you did, there would be no need to hope for it. In the meantime, your responsibility is to get to know God as well as you can and to grow in the process of learning to obey him. It's a wonderful hope and it's worth waiting for.

64

Hope for Victory over Death

When the perishable has been clothed with the imperishable, and the mortal with immortality, then the saying that is written will come true: "Death has been swallowed up in victory."

"Where, O death, is your victory?
Where, O death, is your sting?"

1 Corinthians 15:54–55

Death is a difficult part of life, but it's a necessary part. No one lives forever, as painful as that is. It hurts when you must say goodbye to a loved one who dies. It hurts for a long time. Death happens because humans sinned. It wasn't a part of God's original plan for us.

But because Jesus died to pay the price for humankind's sins, there is hope. When God raised Jesus back to life, he showed his power over death and proved that death doesn't win. It isn't the end. One day all God's followers will be alive in heaven—those who died here on earth and those who are caught up to heaven before they die. Death is defeated!

What a wonderful hope you have. It's okay to be sad when a loved one dies—you're sad because you loved. But don't be without hope. Death is not the end!

65

The Feast Is Coming!

You prepare a table before me
  in the presence of my enemies.
You anoint my head with oil;
  my cup overflows.

PSALM 23:5

Few people get through life without making someone angry once in a while. You may experience criticism or antagonism from others simply because you follow Jesus. Satan will feed their criticism because he will do whatever he can to give you trouble. He wants you to turn away from God.

But the hope of victory is yours because God has your back! He will not allow you to be permanently defeated by your—or his—enemies. What could be more victorious than God preparing a feast for you as a big celebration of the fact that you are part of his family? Your enemies can only stand and watch the party. They can't stop it. They can't join in. They can only watch! How cool is that? While you are feasting at God's table they stand nearby, hungry and frustrated.

God always wins, and because he is protecting and guarding you, you always win too. There may be times when it doesn't feel like you're winning. Victory may seem far off, but be patient and trust God. Keep your fork in hand because the party is coming!

66

Getting through Stress

Cast all your anxiety on him because he cares for you.
1 PETER 5:7

Worry, fear, and anxiety all affect you in some way. These effects show in different ways with everyone. When some people get worried they sleep all the time. Others can't sleep at all. Some eat junk food nonstop. Others can't eat anything. Some function normally and keep everything inside. Others cannot function at all and cry constantly.

Is there a better way to handle anxiety and worry? Yes, give it to God. Just tell him what's worrying you, and ask him to take care of it. Will he fix the problem? Maybe not, but he will give you the necessary strength to face it. God can help you get through stress without losing sleep or gaining (or losing) weight. His presence gives you the assurance that everything is going to be okay. You may have to intentionally give the problem to God daily or hourly—not because he doesn't help you, but because you keep grabbing it back to worry about. Each time it pops into your mind, give it to God and ask for his help. He will calm you and help you fight the worry.

God does this not because he has to but because he loves you.

67

Hope for When You're Tired

He gives strength to the weary
and increases the power of the weak.

ISAIAH 40:29

Sometimes you just get tired of fighting. It feels like life piles on one problem after another. It takes all your energy to get up in the morning and do what you have to do for the day. Maybe you work to put on a good front because of your Christianity. You don't want to let anyone know that you're struggling or hurting. After all, Christians aren't supposed to have problems, right? Wrong. Christians do have struggles, and it's not a negative testament to your faith when you do. On the contrary, struggles are inevitable, and they are an opportunity to reach out to God for help. They are a training ground to help your faith grow stronger.

When you ask God for help he enhances your strength to keep on keeping on through whatever you're dealing with. God will give you strength to face each new day . . . one at a time. You probably won't experience a feeling of superhero strength, like you could fight off the world, but moment-by-moment and problem-by-problem, you'll have what you need. Trust God and thank him for his help.

68

Heartsongs of Music

I will sing to the LORD all my life;
   I will sing praise to my God as long as I live.
May my meditation be pleasing to him,
   as I rejoice in the LORD.

PSALM 104:33–34

Music can play an important role in your spiritual life. You might sing songs of joy when you're happy, silly songs when you feel goofy, and tender songs when you're sad. Music speaks to a place in the soul that plain words don't reach.

Sing out your praises to God! Sing loud and long, whether you can carry a tune or not. Sing thanks for his love for you, for his guidance, for his protection! Sing of his greatness and power! Sing your worship to him.

Sing your requests to God because you know he hears your musical prayers. Sing from the depths of pain in your heart. Sing your cries for rescue and your assurance of his hiding places. Sing because you know his Word to be true.

If there are no existing songs that say what you are feeling, make up your own. Just let your heart sing to him.

Sing to him all your life. Never let your songs of praise and love end. Know that he hears and he takes pleasure in your worship—in your joy and in your requests.

69

Hope for a Purposeful Life

Therefore, my dear friends, as you have always obeyed—not only in my presence, but now much more in my absence—continue to work out your salvation with fear and trembling, for it is God who works in you to will and to act in order to fulfill his good purpose.

PHILIPPIANS 2:12–13

Anything really worth having is worth working for. Think about when you start a diet, not just to lose weight but to be healthy too. When you first start, you're filled with enthusiasm and great intentions. But as time passes some of that enthusiasm fades, and it begins to feel like work to maintain a healthy diet. Still, in your heart you know that the goal of being healthy is a good one, and you should keep pushing through the discouragement and make it work.

What about learning to live for God in obedience and submission? When you first met Jesus you probably enthusiastically embraced the new life he offered and vowed to learn and grow. But along the way you have encountered stumbling blocks and perhaps discouragement. The apostle Paul encourages you not to give up, because a life of obedience to God is worth having. That means it's worth diligently pursuing. God helps you to grow and learn because he has a purpose for your life, and through your obedience and growth that purpose will become more obvious. A life of knowing and serving God creates a life of purpose and meaning.

70

Hope for Restoration

The God of all grace, who called you to his eternal glory in Christ, after you have suffered a little while, will himself restore you and make you strong, firm and steadfast.

1 Peter 5:10

Restored furniture is old furniture that has already lived a life but is given new life. It needs repair or a new coat of paint to make it usable and to give it a fresh look.

People need restoring sometimes too. The stresses of life can beat you down. Heavy problems bruise and wound you. You may come pretty close to being completely broken by what you deal with every day. The suffering may go on for a long time, and you may be tempted to lose hope of ever being out from under its crushing weight. But don't give up hope.

Why must you go through such pain? Only God knows. But you can know with certainty that you are never alone in your suffering. You belong to God, and he is paying attention to all that you're struggling with. Keep calling out to him and trusting him for help. Remember God's promise to rescue you and to restore you in strength and resilience so that you will have new life and usefulness to him.

71

Hope for Wisdom

The LORD gives wisdom;
from his mouth come knowledge and under-
standing.

How often have you mentally played back a conversation you've had and wondered whether you said the right thing . . . or realized that you didn't but wished you had known the right thing to say? If only you had wisdom to give great advice and always speak correctly to others. If only . . .

There's hope for you to gain wisdom. Your heavenly Father is wisdom itself. He created wisdom. His wisdom is available to you through studying his Word . . . ingesting it so that it becomes a part of your heart and thoughts. As you begin to live out his wisdom it will become a part of your normal thoughts, and you can share it with others.

God's wisdom is different than the world's wisdom because of his ability to see the bigger picture of life and his focus on helping you learn to show his love to others. Ask him to give you his wisdom, and spend time in Scripture, letting his Word sink into your heart. That's how you have the hope of great wisdom to share with others and reflect God's love to all.

72

Hope for Peace

Now may the Lord of peace himself give you peace at all times and in every way. The Lord be with all of you.

2 THESSALONIANS 3:16

Peace. Who doesn't want peace? But it's such a fleeting thing, so easily pushed away by anxious thoughts and conflicts. It seems that to be alive in these days is to be bombarded with less than peaceful situations and thoughts. The more people you care about, the more opportunities there are for peace to be distant as you see their struggles. The world is certainly not a peaceful place, and concern for its future can attack your personal peace too.

Is the reality of peace hopeless? No, it isn't, but it surely doesn't come without trusting God and asking him to help you see beyond your current crises. Echo the request in this verse for God to give you peace at all times and in every way. Be still and rest in him. Meditate on his Word. Give him your concerns, and every time you are tempted to grab them back so you can worry on them, give them to him again. He is always with you, loving you and caring for you. He himself is the essence of peace, and he will share that peace with you if you allow him to.

73

God's Best

To the faithful you show yourself faithful,
  to the blameless you show yourself blameless,
to the pure you show yourself pure,
  but to the devious you show yourself shrewd.
You save the humble
  but bring low those whose eyes are haughty.

PSALM 18:25–27

It's a given fact that you do not deserve the grace of God or the gifts of his salvation and blessings. You are a sinner saved by grace, so your salvation and all the blessings he gives you are purely because of his grace and love.

His special blessings are given to those who accept Jesus as their Savior and who focus their energy on living for him and learning to know him in a deeper way. Those who are faithful to him see his faithfulness, those who obey him see his justice, and those who strive to be obedient see his grace.

But people who do not seek to obey or honor God will not, in the long run, see his kindness, only his judgment.

Do you hope to see more of God's goodness and blessing in your life? Then live humbly, giving him credit for all you are and all you have. Don't be filled with pride that pushes God aside and claims its own credit for all good things. If you hope to know God more deeply and enjoy his best, honor him and focus your life on knowing and obeying him.

74

Serving Jesus

Just as you received Christ Jesus as Lord, continue to live your lives in him, rooted and built up in him, strengthened in the faith as you were taught, and overflowing with thankfulness.

COLOSSIANS 2:6–7

When you are learning something new, such as how to drive a car, there's a learning curve until you've learned all you need to know to be ready to drive on your own. Even once you have your license, there are situations you must continue to learn how to maneuver through.

When you receive Jesus as your Savior, you hope for opportunities to serve him even though you don't yet know all you need to know about obeying God and serving him. The Christian life is a journey, so you keep learning and growing. But do you have to reach a certain point before you can feel that you are ready to serve him and actually call yourself a Christian? Of course not. From the moment you accept

Jesus, you are God's child and should begin serving him immediately.

It's true that life with Jesus is a journey and you will always be learning about him, but from the moment you accept him you can begin telling others about his love. So don't put things on hold until you feel you've "arrived"; just get busy living for Jesus. As you serve him and grow more in love with him, your heart will overflow with thankfulness!

75

Hope for Defeating Fear

There is no fear in love. But perfect love drives out fear, because fear has to do with punishment. The one who fears is not made perfect in love.

Fear is crippling. It keeps you from taking risks, which keeps you from having new experiences. Fear can even keep you from doing the things you were once comfortable doing. Fear keeps you in a box where you think you're safe and protected, but it also prevents you from enjoying things you used to enjoy. Once fear has taken hold in your heart, it grows, making your fear spread to other areas.

How do you combat fear? Is there some way to push it away? This verse tells you that there is no fear in love. So your hope for getting rid of fear is to let God's love settle deep in your heart. Make his love your refuge so that any time fear begins to raise its ugly head, you can call on God to remind you of his powerful love. Fear and love cannot both reside in the same place. It's one or the other. If your heart is assured of God's love for you, then there is no room for fear. Your hope for overcoming fear is to realize God's love, accept it, believe it, and trust it.

76

Blessings of Obeying

Blessed are those who keep his statutes
and seek him with all their heart.

PSALM 119:2

The pathway to living for God is often called the straight and narrow. That sounds foreboding, like it's a way of living that's full of rules you have to keep, and that idea keeps some people from wanting to follow God. They think it sounds like their lives would be too limited and confined. That's a shame because living for God and walking the straight and narrow is not at all keeping a list of rules. God's way of living is life-giving because he asks you to live in a way that is good for your life and for the people around you. Living the way God directs makes your life more fulfilling and your relationships with others more pleasant. You learn to treat others with respect and kindness while still obeying and honoring God.

Keeping God's commandments and making the effort to know him in a deeper and more meaningful way lead to blessings from him. You'll experience the blessings of stronger faith, more confidence in your relationship with him, and a deeper understanding of his love for you and of his purpose for your life.

77

Hope for Sure Feet

The Sovereign LORD is my strength;
he makes my feet like the feet of a deer,
he enables me to tread on the heights.

HABAKKUK 3:19

Picking your way through the struggles of life takes some skill. Sometimes you may feel like you're climbing a tall, rocky mountain, and every step you take puts you in danger of slipping from a ledge and plummeting down the mountainside.

However, when you call on the Lord to guide your steps, you have the hope of making it to the peak of the mountain, never once slipping. Your steps will be sure because God is directing you.

You know that God loves you and that his power and strength are greater than any situation you may encounter. He sees the entire picture of your life and knows what's ahead for you. He knows how this current struggle will end and what you can learn from it. Then why is it so difficult to trust him? Perhaps it's because it feels like you're stepping into the unknown. You can't see where you're going, and you're never sure that you're not going to slip. Your trust in God isn't strong enough. But each time you see his protection in your life, you will trust him a little more. His strength will make your steps sure. He won't let you fall.

78

Hope for Equipping

God is able to bless you abundantly, so that in all things at all times, having all that you need, you will abound in every good work.

2 CORINTHIANS 9:8

When God gives you a job to do you may feel that you're not equipped. That you can't possibly do what he wants. There were a few people in the Bible who said "I can't" to God. They were wrong though, because when he asks you to do something, he gives you what you need to accomplish the task. He may not give all the skills at once but a step at a time, as you need them. All he wants you to do is accept the mission he gives you and trust him to bless you with what you need.

Do you desire to serve God? Do you hope to do amazing things for him? Then say yes to whatever he asks you to do, and trust him to supply whatever you need. Remember that he did that for Moses when he asked him to lead his people out of Egypt. He did that for Joshua when he asked him to capture Jericho. God's blessings are abundant, and he will give you all you need in order to do all he asks you to do. Don't be afraid. Don't be timid. Trust him.

79

Material Blessings?

Observe what the LORD your God requires: Walk in obedience to him, and keep his decrees and commands, his laws and regulations, as written in the Law of Moses. Do this so that you may prosper in all you do and wherever you go.

1 KINGS 2:3

Of course you want to prosper in life. Who doesn't? There is the hope that as you mature, your life will get better, and you will have a higher income and a nicer home . . . a more comfortable life. But is that what this verse promises you? Is it saying that if you are obedient to God and follow his laws, he will give you more material things? No, it's not about material blessings at all.

Do you hope for God's best in your life? Then don't think about his best as financial blessings. God's best for you is better than money or nice homes or cars. It is for you to know him deeply and trust him more fully. Your relationship with him and your growth to become more like Christ are the most important things to him.

That's what this verse is saying—obey God. Keep his commands and laws. Then you are honoring and obeying him and learning to be more like Christ—obedient to God, a humble servant, loving others more than yourself. If you live that way, you will indeed prosper in God's sight and receive his blessing of more opportunities to serve him.

80

Hope in Nourishment

Blessed is the one who trusts in the Lord,
*   whose confidence is in him.*
They will be like a tree planted by the water
*   that sends out its roots by the stream.*
It does not fear when heat comes;
*   its leaves are always green.*
It has no worries in a year of drought
*   and never fails to bear fruit.*

JEREMIAH 17:7–8

In a time of drought, plants and trees starve. As the drought persists, water dries up, and even trees with deep roots begin to struggle to get enough nourishment. But a tree that's even somewhat near a river will send its roots out toward the stream until it can locate water so the entire tree can get what it needs to survive. The whole tree—trunk, branches, and leaves—depends on the work of the roots to survive.

Your trust in God is your only hope of survival in a world that continuously tries to pull you away from him. Putting your trust in him over anything else is like a tree root seeking water from a stream and supplying all the needs of the entire plant. Your trust in God gives you everything you need to resist the temptations of Satan. It gives you the nourishment to grow in your faith, and it feeds your strength to love others and to live humbly before God. You just can't do all of this in your own strength. Your energy will dry up, and you will die. Only with the nourishment of trusting God can you survive.

81

Hope from Discipline

Blessed is the one whom God corrects.

JOB 5:17

Being corrected is no fun. Correction is discipline, and you're only disciplined when you've done something wrong. When you disobey a rule that your parents gave you or the rules of the road when you're driving, you are subject to discipline. It's not a bad thing to be disciplined; it helps you remember to obey the rules, and that makes life in the family more pleasant and the roads and highways safer.

In your hope to grow more like Christ there will be times when God disciplines you. His discipline takes various forms. Sometimes it comes through another Christian challenging you about choices you're making. Sometimes it comes through lost opportunities. Sometimes it comes through a feeling deep in your heart.

It's important to remember that God only disciplines you because he loves you. He wants very good things for you, and he knows that it's necessary for you to obey him and follow his Word in order to have the best life possible.

So if you hope for the best life with God, accept his discipline, learn what you must from it, move forward with the new lesson learned, and thank him for his love that cares enough to discipline.

82

Hope for the Faithful

These were all commended for their faith, yet none of them re-
ceived what had been promised, since God had planned some-
thing better for us so that only together with us would they be
made perfect.

Hebrews 11 lists great heroes of the faith and records the amazing ways they honored God by their faith in him. Their inspirational stories provide wonderful examples of trusting God and living for him. God was pleased with them, and he made sure they were included in this Hall of Faith chapter.

Interestingly, none of them were immediately rewarded for their lives of faith. They lived obedient lives and served God, yet they didn't get the reward God promised. Why not? Because their stories wouldn't be complete without yours. Their faith and your faith come together for a beautiful reward in heaven. You learn from the way they served God, and they are witnesses to how you serve him. They are the crowd of witnesses in heaven watching your faith and trust in God grow stronger and stronger! Your life of faith makes theirs more complete, and theirs make yours complete. So you will share in the grand reward of heaven together with them. How wonderful to be part of the entire family of God.

83

Hope in God Showing Up

The sun stopped in the middle of the sky and delayed going down about a full day. There has never been a day like it before or since, a day when the LORD listened to a human being. Surely the LORD was fighting for Israel!

JOSHUA 10:13–14

Joshua's army was fighting a battle that he really wanted to win, so he asked God to make the sun stand still—to prolong the daylight hours so his army could defeat God's enemies. What an amazing request. What's even more amazing is that God did it! He made the sun stand still in the sky so Joshua's army could defeat their enemies. As these verses say, that had never happened before and has never happened since.

Do you need God's help with something so big you know there is no other hope for a way to handle it, no logical way for the problem to be solved? It's going to take God's miraculous strength to deal with it. Do you dare ask him for a miracle? Will he hear your request?

You have the certain hope of God hearing what you ask. How he chooses to handle your crisis is, of course, up to him, but you can be assured he will hear and he will help. You never know how God will show up for you, but you can always be certain that he will show up in some way, and it will be exciting!

84

Hope in Your Importance to God

The very hairs of your head are all numbered. Don't be afraid; you are worth more than many sparrows.

LUKE 12:7

Do you feel that perhaps your requests are too small and unimportant compared to what others deal with? God has so much to take care of. Really—there are wars around the world, people dying from thirst or starvation, children suffering. Homeless people and sick veterans must take up a lot of God's time. There are massive storms and earthquakes and then the everyday occurrences of illness, death, or broken relationships. He is constantly bombarded with cries for help.

Maybe God doesn't need to be bothered with your problems. Of course you know he loves you, but maybe you feel you shouldn't ask him to handle your mundane requests.

It may be tempting to feel that way, but it isn't true. God is big enough to handle all the problems of the world and to hear every prayer as it is being uttered. He cares about you. He cares so much that he has counted the very hairs on your head! You're worth that much to him! So ask him what you need to ask him. Tell him what you want to tell him. Bask in his love and care for you.

85

Where Is Your Treasure?

Do not store up for yourselves treasures on earth, where moths and vermin destroy, and where thieves break in and steal. But store up for yourselves treasures in heaven, where moths and vermin do not destroy, and where thieves do not break in and steal. For where your treasure is, there your heart will be also.

MATTHEW 6:19–21

You may say all the right words about loving and honoring God, and that is good. But words without action behind them are just that—words. You need more than words to show where your heart is truly focused. Where do you put your time? Where do you invest your finances? What takes up most of your thoughts and conversations? Those things indicate where your treasure is. They are the proof of what's truly important to you.

Your hope is the certainty of heaven where you will spend eternity. What you invest in that future will be your reward. Do you need to take a step back and evaluate where your treasure really is? Be careful about what's important to you here on earth. You won't get a chance to redo those time and energy investments once you leave this earth. Show God that he is truly your priority. Invest your energy, time, finances, thoughts—everything—in his work on earth. Your heart will then be focused on serving and honoring him, and your treasure will be in heaven.

86

Praise to Almighty God!

To him who is able to keep you from stumbling and to present you before his glorious presence without fault and with great joy—to the only God our Savior be glory, majesty, power and authority, through Jesus Christ our Lord, before all ages, now and forevermore! Amen.

JUDE 24–25

The only hope you have to make it through the struggles of this life and stay true to God is to call on him for help. He can keep you from giving in to temptation that would pull you away from living for him. His strength in you can keep you true to obeying him. His power and authority will defeat any other power or person on earth. He is God Almighty, and because you are his child, that power is available to you for the asking. You need only to be submissive to his guidance and to his plan for your life.

The blessing of that hope is that you will one day stand before him fault-free, your sin cleaned up by the blood of

Jesus, and God himself will celebrate with joy because you are there with him.

So praise him now! Praise God for his glory, majesty, power, and authority over everything! Praise him for his unending, unconditional, sacrificial love for you! His love is the reason you can have any hope at all. It gives you hope for all eternity.

87

Hope in Keeping On

I want to know Christ—yes, to know the power of his resurrection and participation in his sufferings, becoming like him in his death, and so, somehow, attaining to the resurrection from the dead. Not that I have already obtained all this, or have already arrived at my goal, but I press on to take hold of that for which Christ Jesus took hold of me.

PHILIPPIANS 3:10–12

Keep on keeping on. That's the message Paul shares. Keep on keeping on toward the goal you hope for. What's important to you? What are you willing to sacrifice, to leave behind, to suffer for? You won't keep pressing toward a goal if it's not the most important thing to you.

Hopefully you, like Paul, are pressing toward achieving the goal Christ has set for you. He wants your full submission—a heart and mind that are totally dedicated to him and willing to obey, regardless of how difficult it sometimes is. He wants your attitude of service to be "I'll go where you want me to go, and I'll do what you want me to do." Is that your attitude even when you don't understand why he is asking you to do something or to go somewhere? Do you trust him enough to step out in darkness, knowing he will set your feet on solid ground?

Faith is a day-by-day journey. It's a learning process and not one that comes quickly or easily. You must commit to it every day—sometimes multiple times a day—in order to keep your eyes on the goal of knowing and serving God.

88

Hope in His Protection

You are my refuge and my shield;
I have put my hope in your word.
PSALM 119:114

G od is your refuge—your place of protection from danger and wickedness. He goes before you, he comes behind you, he hems you in on all sides. He is your shield against all attacks. Satan tries everything he can think of to discourage your connection to God and to convince you that God doesn't care about you, that he doesn't matter, or even that he isn't real. Your mind knows it's not true, but sometimes your heart needs a respite from the doubts. Let God shield you while the bruises on your heart heal and your strength to stand for him returns.

Think about a shield as a deflector. When someone shoots unkind, critical words at you that make you doubt your worth, the shield of the truth of God's Word deflects them away from your heart. The truth of who he says you are to him is protected. God's Word is truth, and what you learn from it will help you to know God better and to guide you in living for him.

Your hope for safety and protection is in God and his Word. Keep them at the forefront of your thoughts at all times.

89

Hope in Community

Though one may be overpowered,
two can defend themselves.
A cord of three strands is not quickly broken.

ECCLESIASTES 4:12

It's a good thing to have friends, and it's a blessing to have the right friends. The right friends are those who share your faith in Jesus and who will hold you accountable to living for him. They aren't afraid to challenge you about choices you make or whether you're living your life in obedience to God's Word. This kind of friend will stand with you against attacks from others or from Satan himself. Holding each other up in prayer and with words of encouragement gives you the power and strength to stand against all kinds of attacks. Together you are twice as strong. Your bond of friendship and faith is unbreakable.

Three cords are referred to in this verse. You and your friend are two of the cords. What's the third cord? Christ himself! He is always standing with you against attacks and in the battles of life. God in his wisdom knows that while Christ is enough, sometimes you need someone with skin on to stand next to you and hold you up with words of encouragement and pats on the back. In this way, you and your friend are braided together with Christ. That is a cord that nothing and no one can break!

90

Hope for a Rich Life

The love of money is a root of all kinds of evil. Some people, eager for money, have wandered from the faith and pierced themselves with many griefs.

1 TIMOTHY 6:10

Money isn't evil. If God has blessed you with a goodly amount of it, then praise him! Use it to do good things for his kingdom and his people. But . . . don't *love* money. When you love money more than you love God, working to get more money becomes most important. You may even be tempted to cheat or steal to get more money. That's where wandering from the faith comes in. Those who put their focus on money push aside living for God and obeying him. They forget about helping those who don't have enough to live on and about God's work around the world that needs financial support. They focus their generosity where a tax write-off is involved so their "generosity" benefits them.

If you are money focused, you're hurting yourself. You will, in the long run, cause yourself grief by your disobedience to God. You will answer to him for it.

Make knowing and serving God the most important thing in your life. Live generously with all he gives you. You will have the hope of the reward you gain. To hear "Well done, my good and faithful servant" is worth more than money in the bank!

Carolyn Larsen is the bestselling author of more than fifty books for children and adults. She has been a speaker for women's events and classes around the world, bringing scriptural messages filled with humor and tenderness. For more information, visit carolynlarsen.com and follow her on Facebook.

Connect with
Carolyn

Author Photo: Bennorth Images of St. Charles, IL

CAROLYNLARSEN.COM

Carolyn Larsen

Find *Comfort* through the Promises in God's Word

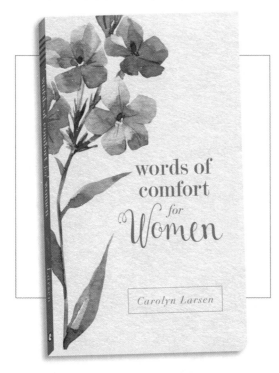

A 90-day devotional that encourages you during the challenges of life, offering comfort through the promises in God's Word and the people he places in your path.